# The Cosmic Connection
# Astrology as a Tool
# for Spiritual Growth
## Seraphina Hartwell

copyright © 2012 Seraphina Hartwell

All rights reserved.

ISBN:**ISBN:** 9798317377656

# DEDICATION

For Mum and Dad.
I have done it with
Your Inspiration

# ACKNOWLEDGMENTS

Them that I love,
know that I love them.
This time I want to
thank my readers,
who have gone through my books
and created Inspiration
for growth together.

# CONTENTS

Introduction: Bridging Heaven and Earth .................................................. 3

1: Astrology as a Spiritual Language and Tool – More Than Just Horoscopes ........................................................................................... 6

2: Understanding Your Birth Chart – A Map of Your Soul ........................ 11

3: Planetary Energies and Spiritual Growth – The Spiritual Meaning of Transits ................................................................................................... 22

4: Moon Cycles and Emotional Healing – Aligning with Lunar Energy ....... 25

5: Using Astrology for Self-Reflection and Growth ................................... 28

6: The Role of Retrogrades in Spiritual Lessons ...................................... 32

Conclusion: Embracing the Cosmic Dance .............................................. 35

ABOUT THE AUTHOR ............................... **Error! Bookmark not defined.**

# INTRODUCTION: BRIDGING HEAVEN AND EARTH

The night sky has always held an unspoken promise—a whisper of connection to something greater than ourselves. Gazing upward at the tapestry of stars, it's easy to feel both infinitesimally small and profoundly significant all at once. For centuries, humanity has looked to the heavens for guidance, seeking answers in the patterns of constellations, the rhythmic dance of planets, and the silent pull of cosmic forces. Yet somewhere along the way, astrology became relegated to newspaper horoscopes and fleeting memes—dismissed as mere entertainment rather than the profound spiritual tool it truly is.

But what if astrology were more than just a source of daily predictions or superficial personality traits? What if it could serve as a bridge between our inner worlds and the vast expanse of the universe, offering insights into who we are, why we're here, and how we can navigate life's twists and turns with grace and purpose?

This book invites you to step beyond the surface-level interpretations of sun signs and delve into the deeper mysteries of astrology as a language of the soul. Here, astrology is not about fortune-telling; it's about self-discovery. It's not about predicting outcomes but understanding processes. It's not about controlling fate but aligning with the natural flow of existence. Through this lens, astrology becomes a mirror reflecting your deepest truths and a compass guiding you toward growth, healing, and transformation.

In these pages, we will explore how the positions of celestial bodies at the moment of your birth create a unique blueprint—a map of your soul—that reveals your strengths, challenges, desires, and potential. We'll uncover the spiritual significance of planetary movements, known as transits, which act as catalysts for change and evolution. We'll examine the emotional tides governed by the moon's cycles and learn how to harness their energy for healing and manifestation. And we'll demystify retrogrades, those often-feared periods that actually offer invaluable opportunities for reflection and recalibration.

Astrology, when approached with intention and reverence, becomes far more than a system of symbols and calculations. It becomes a living practice—a means of connecting with the divine intelligence woven into the fabric of creation. Whether you're navigating a major life transition, seeking clarity during times of confusion, or simply yearning to understand yourself on a deeper level, astrology offers tools to illuminate your path.

Who is this journey meant for? Perhaps you've dabbled in astrology before, reading your horoscope out of curiosity or fascination. Maybe you've felt drawn to the mystical allure of the cosmos but didn't know where to begin. Or maybe you're someone who senses there's more to astrology than meets the eye and longs to unlock its hidden wisdom. Whoever you are, wherever you find yourself on your spiritual quest, this book is designed to meet you where you are and guide you forward.

# INTRODUCTION: BRIDGING HEAVEN AND EARTH

The night sky has always held an unspoken promise—a whisper of connection to something greater than ourselves. Gazing upward at the tapestry of stars, it's easy to feel both infinitesimally small and profoundly significant all at once. For centuries, humanity has looked to the heavens for guidance, seeking answers in the patterns of constellations, the rhythmic dance of planets, and the silent pull of cosmic forces. Yet somewhere along the way, astrology became relegated to newspaper horoscopes and fleeting memes—dismissed as mere entertainment rather than the profound spiritual tool it truly is.

But what if astrology were more than just a source of daily predictions or superficial personality traits? What if it could serve as a bridge between our inner worlds and the vast expanse of the universe, offering insights into who we are, why we're here, and how we can navigate life's twists and turns with grace and purpose?

This book invites you to step beyond the surface-level interpretations of sun signs and delve into the deeper mysteries of astrology as a language of the soul. Here, astrology is not about fortune-telling; it's about self-discovery. It's not about predicting outcomes but understanding processes. It's not about controlling fate but aligning with the natural flow of existence. Through this lens, astrology becomes a mirror reflecting your deepest truths and a compass guiding you toward growth, healing, and transformation.

In these pages, we will explore how the positions of celestial bodies at the moment of your birth create a unique blueprint—a map of your soul—that reveals your strengths, challenges, desires, and potential. We'll uncover the spiritual significance of planetary movements, known as transits, which act as catalysts for change and evolution. We'll examine the emotional tides governed by the moon's cycles and learn how to harness their energy for healing and manifestation. And we'll demystify retrogrades, those often-feared periods that actually offer invaluable opportunities for reflection and recalibration.

Astrology, when approached with intention and reverence, becomes far more than a system of symbols and calculations. It becomes a living practice—a means of connecting with the divine intelligence woven into the fabric of creation. Whether you're navigating a major life transition, seeking clarity during times of confusion, or simply yearning to understand yourself on a deeper level, astrology offers tools to illuminate your path.

Who is this journey meant for? Perhaps you've dabbled in astrology before, reading your horoscope out of curiosity or fascination. Maybe you've felt drawn to the mystical allure of the cosmos but didn't know where to begin. Or maybe you're someone who senses there's more to astrology than meets the eye and longs to unlock its hidden wisdom. Whoever you are, wherever you find yourself on your spiritual quest, this book is designed to meet you where you are and guide you forward.

# The Cosmic Connection Astrology as a Tool for Spiritual Growth

As you embark on this exploration, I encourage you to approach astrology not as a passive observer but as an active participant. Use the exercises, reflections, and insights within these chapters to engage deeply with the material. Create rituals, track transits, and listen closely to the whispers of your own intuition. Let astrology be both a teacher and a companion as you traverse the terrain of your inner world and its connection to the cosmos.

Together, we will unravel the threads that bind heaven and earth, discovering how the movements of distant planets echo the rhythms of our hearts and minds. By the end of this journey, my hope is that you will see astrology not merely as a tool but as a sacred art—one that empowers you to live in harmony with the universe and embrace the fullness of your being.

So take a deep breath, open your heart, and prepare to step into the cosmic dance. The stars have stories to tell, and they are waiting for you to listen.

## 1: ASTROLOGY AS A SPIRITUAL LANGUAGE AND TOOL – MORE THAN JUST HOROSCOPES

The room was quiet except for the soft hum of rain tapping against the windowpane. Sarah sat cross-legged on her worn-out couch, a steaming mug of chamomile tea cradled in her hands. Her laptop glowed faintly before her, casting warm light onto her face as she scrolled through yet another article titled "What Your Sun Sign Says About You." She sighed, leaning back into the cushions. The words felt hollow—like they were skimming the surface of something vast and mysterious without ever diving beneath.

For years, astrology had been nothing more than a guilty pleasure for Sarah. She'd check her horoscope occasionally, giggling at how eerily accurate it sometimes seemed—or rolling her eyes when it missed the mark entirely. But lately, there was an ache inside her, a yearning for meaning that no meme or one-liner could satisfy. Something about the stars called to her—not just as entertainment but as a doorway to understanding herself and the world around her.

# The Cosmic Connection Astrology as a Tool for Spiritual Growth

She closed her laptop abruptly, setting it aside. "There has to be more," she muttered aloud, staring out the rain-speckled window. And then, almost instinctively, her gaze shifted upward toward the night sky peeking through breaks in the clouds. It wasn't the first time she'd wondered if those distant lights held secrets meant just for her.

Astrology, contrary to popular belief, is not merely a collection of zodiac memes or daily predictions printed alongside weather forecasts. At its core, astrology is a spiritual language—an ancient system of symbols and archetypes that bridges the gap between the human experience and the infinite cosmos. To reduce it to sun signs and horoscopes is like mistaking a single brushstroke for the entire painting. True astrology delves far deeper, offering a framework for understanding ourselves, our relationships, and even the unfolding cycles of history.

Imagine the universe as a grand symphony, each planet playing its own unique instrument. The sun represents vitality and identity, shining brightly as the conductor of this celestial orchestra. The moon sways with emotion, pulling tides within us as much as it does across oceans. Mercury races ahead, quick-witted and curious, while Venus sings softly of love and beauty. Mars marches forward with determination, igniting passion and action. Jupiter expands boundaries, Saturn teaches discipline, Uranus disrupts norms, Neptune dissolves illusions, and Pluto transforms all it touches.

These planetary energies are not abstract concepts; they are alive within us, shaping our personalities, influencing our decisions, and guiding our paths. When we begin to see astrology as a reflection of universal principles rather than mere fortune-telling, we unlock its true power: the ability to connect with something greater than ourselves.

# The Cosmic Connection Astrology as a Tool for Spiritual Growth

Sarah's journey into astrology began innocently enough. A friend had casually mentioned once that knowing your rising sign could reveal aspects of your personality beyond what your sun sign showed. Intrigued, Sarah decided to look up hers. What she found startled her. While her sun sign (Libra) explained her desire for balance and harmony, her rising sign (Scorpio) illuminated the intensity and depth she often kept hidden from others. Suddenly, pieces of herself clicked into place—traits she'd always struggled to articulate now made sense.

But the real turning point came when Sarah attended a workshop led by an astrologer named Maya. With silver-streaked hair and a voice as soothing as waves lapping against the shore, Maya spoke of astrology not as a predictive tool but as a map of the soul. "Your birth chart," she said, holding up a circular diagram filled with lines and symbols, "is like a cosmic fingerprint. No two charts are alike, just as no two souls are identical."

Maya went on to explain how the positions of the planets at the exact moment of someone's birth create a snapshot of the heavens—a blueprint that reveals their potential, challenges, and purpose. As Sarah listened, her skepticism melted away, replaced by a growing sense of wonder. For the first time, astrology didn't feel like a parlor trick; it felt like truth.

Afterward, during the Q&A session, Sarah raised her hand hesitantly. "How do you know where to start?" she asked. "It feels overwhelming."

Maya smiled warmly. "Start with curiosity," she replied. "Think of astrology as a conversation with the universe. Ask questions, observe patterns, and trust your intuition. Over time, the answers will come."

# The Cosmic Connection Astrology as a Tool for Spiritual Growth

To understand astrology as a spiritual tool, it's essential to move beyond the oversimplifications perpetuated by mainstream culture. Yes, sun signs offer valuable insights into core identity, but they represent only one piece of the puzzle. Each element of a natal chart—the houses, planets, signs, aspects, and angles—adds layers of complexity, painting a multidimensional portrait of the individual.

Consider the twelve houses of astrology, which divide life into distinct areas such as career, relationships, health, and spirituality. These houses act as stages upon which the planets perform their roles. For example, someone with Venus (the planet of love) in the seventh house might find fulfillment through partnerships, while another person with Mars (the planet of drive) in the tenth house may channel their ambition into professional success.

Then there are aspects—the geometric relationships between planets— which reveal how different energies interact. A harmonious trine suggests ease and flow, while a challenging square indicates tension and growth opportunities. Understanding these dynamics allows us to work with our chart rather than against it, using astrology as a guide for personal evolution.

That evening, after the workshop, Sarah couldn't stop thinking about what Maya had said. She pulled out her phone and downloaded an app recommended by the astrologer, entering her birth details carefully. When her chart appeared—a kaleidoscope of colors and symbols—she stared at it in awe. It looked complicated, yes, but also deeply personal, like a secret code waiting to be deciphered.

## The Cosmic Connection Astrology as a Tool for Spiritual Growth

Her finger hovered over the screen as she traced the lines connecting the planets. There was so much to unpack, so many stories woven into the fabric of her being. Yet instead of feeling overwhelmed, Sarah felt excited. For the first time in a long time, she had a tangible starting point—a way to explore the questions that had lingered in her heart for years.

"What am I here to learn?" she whispered to herself, gazing at the chart. "And how can I grow?"

Little did she know, the answers would unfold gradually, like petals opening under the morning sun. Astrology wouldn't give her instant solutions—it rarely works that way—but it would provide a roadmap, illuminating the twists and turns of her journey. And as Sarah took her first steps into this cosmic terrain, she realized something profound: the universe wasn't separate from her. It was speaking directly to her, through the language of the stars.

In the chapters ahead, we'll delve deeper into the mechanics of astrology, beginning with the natal chart—a sacred map of the soul—and exploring how its components reflect your innermost truths. We'll examine the spiritual significance of planetary transits, uncover the emotional wisdom of the moon's cycles, and learn how to use astrology as a tool for self-reflection and growth. But for now, take a moment to sit with this idea: the cosmos is not indifferent to your existence. It holds you in its embrace, whispering guidance through every alignment, every cycle, every shift in the heavens.

Are you ready to listen?

## 2: UNDERSTANDING YOUR BIRTH CHART – A MAP OF YOUR SOUL

The morning light filtered through Sarah's bedroom window, casting golden streaks across the wooden floor. She sat at her desk, a steaming cup of coffee beside her and an open notebook in front of her. Her laptop displayed the birth chart she'd generated the night before—a swirling mandala of symbols, lines, and colors that seemed both foreign and familiar. It was as if someone had taken the fragmented pieces of her life and arranged them into a cosmic puzzle.

But how to begin? The chart looked overwhelming, like a labyrinth waiting to be navigated. Each symbol felt loaded with meaning, yet deciphering it required patience and focus—qualities Sarah wasn't sure she possessed. Still, she couldn't shake the feeling that this map held answers to questions she hadn't fully articulated yet.

She took a sip of coffee, letting its warmth steady her nerves. "Okay," she whispered to herself, "one step at a time."

# The Cosmic Connection Astrology as a Tool for Spiritual Growth

A natal chart is more than just a snapshot of the sky at the moment of your birth; it's a sacred blueprint of your soul's journey. Imagine standing on Earth at the exact time and place you were born, looking up at the heavens. The positions of the planets, the signs they occupy, and the houses they inhabit create a unique pattern—a celestial fingerprint—that reflects who you are and what you're here to learn.

To understand your birth chart, think of it as a three-tiered system:

1. **Planets**: These represent the actors in your cosmic play. Each planet embodies a specific energy or archetype. For example:

   - The Sun represents your core identity and purpose.

   - The Moon governs your emotions and inner world.

   - Mercury rules communication and thought processes.

   - Venus influences love, beauty, and values.

   - Mars drives action, passion, and ambition.

   - Jupiter expands horizons and brings opportunities.

   - Saturn imposes structure and teaches discipline.

   - Uranus disrupts norms and sparks innovation.

   - Neptune dissolves boundaries and inspires dreams.

   - Pluto transforms and regenerates.

2. **Zodiac Signs**: These describe *how* each planet expresses itself. If planets are actors, then signs are their costumes and scripts. For instance, a fiery Aries Mars might manifest as boldness and impulsivity, while a watery Pisces Venus could express itself through deep compassion and artistic sensitivity.

3. **Houses**: These divide life into twelve distinct arenas, each representing a different area of experience. The house a planet occupies shows where its energy plays out most strongly in your life. For example:

   - The first house (self) relates to identity and appearance.

   - The fourth house (home) pertains to family and roots.

   - The seventh house (partnerships) deals with relationships.

   - The tenth house (career) focuses on public image and achievements.

When these elements come together, they form a rich tapestry of insight into your personality, strengths, challenges, and life path.

---

Sarah began with the basics, starting with her Sun sign. As a Libra, she already knew she valued balance and harmony, often finding herself mediating conflicts between friends or striving to maintain equilibrium in her own life. But seeing the Sun positioned in the fifth house of creativity and self-expression gave her pause. Was there something here she'd been neglecting? Perhaps her need for harmony stemmed not only from her desire to please others but also from a deeper yearning to create beauty and joy.

Next, she turned her attention to her Moon sign. Scorpio. That made sense—it explained the intensity she often felt bubbling beneath the surface, the way emotions could overwhelm her like a tidal wave. Her Moon resided in the twelfth house, the realm of spirituality, solitude, and hidden truths. This placement suggested a soul drawn to introspection and mystery, someone who needed periods of retreat to recharge and process their feelings. No wonder she always craved quiet moments alone after busy days.

As she continued exploring her chart, Sarah stumbled upon her Rising sign—or Ascendant—which represented the mask she wore to the outside world. Scorpio again. So, while her Libra Sun sought peace and cooperation, her Scorpio Rising projected an air of depth and magnetism, drawing people in without revealing too much too soon. It was a fascinating duality, one she recognized immediately. People often described her as warm yet enigmatic, easygoing yet fiercely private. Now she understood why.

Her fingers hovered over the screen as she examined the rest of her chart. There was so much to unpack: Mercury conjunct Venus in Virgo, suggesting precision in communication and a love for detail; Mars in Sagittarius, fueling her adventurous spirit and thirst for freedom; Saturn in Capricorn, instilling a strong work ethic and sense of responsibility. Each piece added another layer to the mosaic of her being.

# The Cosmic Connection Astrology as a Tool for Spiritual Growth

Understanding your birth chart isn't just about memorizing facts or decoding symbols; it's about recognizing patterns and themes that resonate with your lived experience. Take aspects, for example—the geometric angles formed between planets. These reveal how planetary energies interact, creating either harmony or tension.

- **Conjunctions** occur when two planets share the same degree, blending their energies seamlessly. For Sarah, her Mercury-Venus conjunction in Virgo highlighted her natural ability to communicate with kindness and clarity.

- **Squares**, on the other hand, indicate friction and challenge. Her Mars square Neptune aspect suggested struggles with asserting herself clearly, sometimes losing direction amidst idealistic dreams.

- **Trines** represent flow and ease. Her Jupiter trine Uranus connection pointed to sudden bursts of inspiration and luck, especially in areas involving innovation or unconventional paths.

By identifying these dynamics, you can better understand your strengths and navigate your challenges. Astrology doesn't dictate fate; instead, it offers tools for growth, helping you align with your highest potential.

Later that afternoon, Sarah decided to take a walk to clear her head. The crisp autumn air carried the scent of fallen leaves, and the sun hung low in the sky, casting long shadows across the park. She replayed the insights she'd gleaned from her chart, marveling at how they mirrored her reality.

"Hey, stranger!" a voice called out, interrupting her thoughts. Turning, she saw Maya—the astrologer from the workshop—approaching with a friendly smile.

"Maya! What are the chances?" Sarah laughed, genuinely surprised.

"I was hoping I'd run into you," Maya said, falling into step beside her. "How's the chart exploration going?"

"It's... intense," Sarah admitted. "I feel like I'm meeting myself for the first time, even though I've lived with me my whole life."

Maya chuckled knowingly. "That's astrology for you. It has a way of holding up a mirror and saying, 'Here you are.' But remember, it's not about perfection. It's about awareness. Every planet, every sign, every house—they all have gifts and lessons. The key is learning how to dance with them."

They walked in companionable silence for a while before Maya spoke again. "You know, the chart is just the beginning. Once you understand its foundation, you can start applying it to your daily life. Transits, progressions, cycles—they'll show you how the universe supports your growth in real-time."

Sarah nodded thoughtfully. "I'm ready to keep going. Where do I start next?"

Maya smiled. "With the moon. Its phases and rhythms hold incredible power for emotional healing and manifestation. Trust me, once you connect with lunar energy, you'll never see the night sky the same way again."

That evening, as Sarah gazed at the crescent moon hanging low in the sky, she felt a renewed sense of purpose. Her birth chart had opened a door, inviting her to explore not just who she was but who she could become. And though the journey ahead promised challenges, she no longer feared them. After all, the stars weren't distant observers—they were partners in her evolution, whispering encouragement with every turn of the celestial wheel.

In the chapters to come, we'll delve deeper into the spiritual significance of planetary transits, uncover the transformative power of retrogrades, and explore how to align your life with cosmic cycles. But for now, take a moment to sit with your own chart. Let it speak to you, guiding you toward greater self-awareness and alignment with your truest self. The map of your soul awaits—will you follow it?

## 2: UNDERSTANDING YOUR BIRTH CHART – A MAP OF YOUR SOUL

The morning light filtered through Sarah's bedroom window, casting golden streaks across the wooden floor. She sat at her desk, a steaming cup of coffee beside her and an open notebook in front of her. Her laptop displayed the birth chart she'd generated the night before—a swirling mandala of symbols, lines, and colors that seemed both foreign and familiar. It was as if someone had taken the fragmented pieces of her life and arranged them into a cosmic puzzle.

But where to begin? The chart looked overwhelming, like a labyrinth waiting to be explored. Each symbol felt loaded with meaning, yet deciphering it required patience and focus—qualities Sarah wasn't sure she possessed. Still, she couldn't shake the feeling that this map held answers to questions she hadn't fully articulated yet.

She took a sip of coffee, letting its warmth settle her nerves. "Okay," she whispered, "one step at a time."

---

A natal chart is more than a snapshot of the sky at the moment of your birth; it's a sacred blueprint of your soul's purpose. Imagine standing on Earth at the exact time and place you were born, looking up at the heavens. The positions of the planets, the signs they occupy, and the houses they inhabit create a unique pattern—a cosmic fingerprint—that reflects who you are and what you're here to learn.

Think of your birth chart as a three-part system:

1. **Planets**: These are the actors in your life's story, each representing a distinct energy:
   - The Sun: your core identity and vitality
   - The Moon: your emotions and inner world
   - Mercury: communication and thought processes
   - Venus: love, beauty, and values
   - Mars: action, passion, and drive
   - Jupiter: growth and optimism
   - Saturn: discipline and life lessons
   - Uranus: innovation and sudden change
   - Neptune: dreams, intuition, and illusion
   - Pluto: transformation and rebirth
2. **Zodiac Signs**: These describe *how* each planet expresses its energy. If planets are actors, signs are their costumes and character traits. For example, Mars in Aries acts boldly and directly, while Mars in Pisces may act more subtly and with emotion.
3. **Houses**: The twelve houses represent different areas of life—like scenes in a play. Each house shows *where* planetary energy shows up:
   - 1st House: Self and identity
   - 4th House: Home and family
   - 7th House: Relationships and partnerships
   - 10th House: Career and public image

As you begin to interpret your chart, you uncover your strengths, your blind spots, and the themes that will weave through your life.

---

Sarah began with her Sun sign. As a Libra, she valued balance and harmony—she often found herself playing mediator in group settings or navigating her own desire to avoid conflict. But seeing her Sun in the 5th house, the realm of creativity and joy, sparked something new. Maybe her urge for peace wasn't only about avoiding discomfort—it could also reflect a deeper need to create beauty and inspire joy.

Then she examined her Moon. It was in Scorpio, placed in the introspective 12th house. This explained her emotional intensity, her tendency to retreat into solitude, and her connection to dreams and hidden truths. It also revealed her emotional vulnerability and need for spiritual healing.

She moved on to her rising sign—Scorpio again. This confirmed her magnetic presence, her air of mystery, and the deep emotional undercurrents that others sensed but rarely saw. The juxtaposition of a diplomatic Libra Sun with a passionate Scorpio Ascendant intrigued her. She wasn't just seeking harmony—she was also learning how to navigate emotional truth with courage.

---

Understanding a chart also involves aspects—geometric angles between planets that describe how their energies interact. Sarah noticed a conjunction between Mercury and Venus in Virgo, suggesting a precise and thoughtful communication style, especially in matters of love or aesthetics. She also noted a square between Mars and Neptune, pointing to challenges asserting herself clearly—especially when dreams or ideals clouded her direction.

These pieces, once scattered, were beginning to form a picture.

---

Later that day, Sarah took a long walk through a nearby park, turning over her insights. She thought about how often she had tried to be what others needed instead of honoring her emotional truth. How she pursued perfection but often lost herself in the process. Now, seeing those tendencies reflected in her chart, she felt less judged by them—and more empowered to shift them.

In the evening, she called Maya. "This chart is intense," Sarah confessed. "I feel like I'm meeting myself for the first time."

Maya smiled over the phone. "That's astrology's gift. It doesn't define you—it reveals you. And once you understand your blueprint, you can start working with it instead of against it."

---

In the next chapter, we'll explore the impact of planetary transits—how the current movement of planets awakens parts of your natal chart and mirrors your ongoing growth. Astrology isn't static. It's alive. And so are you.

## 3: PLANETARY ENERGIES AND SPIRITUAL GROWTH – THE SPIRITUAL MEANING OF TRANSITS

The clock struck midnight, its chimes echoing softly through Sarah's small apartment. She sat cross-legged on the floor, her laptop glowing dimly in front of her. On the screen was a calendar app synced with astrological data, showing upcoming planetary movements—transits—that would soon sweep across her birth chart like cosmic winds. Her eyes lingered on one date circled in red: Saturn conjunct her natal Sun. It felt heavy, like a storm cloud building on the horizon.

She exhaled slowly, trying to steady herself. "What does it mean?" she murmured, the hum of the city outside her window barely audible.

For weeks, Sarah had been studying transits—the way current planetary positions interact with her natal chart. At first, it all seemed abstract. But then, she noticed patterns. During Mercury retrogrades, miscommunications multiplied. When Jupiter aligned with her Venus, unexpected moments of joy emerged. These weren't coincidences. They were cosmic nudges—signs of a deeper rhythm guiding her growth.

Planetary transits are one of astrology's most dynamic tools. While your birth chart is a snapshot of the sky at the moment you were born, transits are like moving spotlights illuminating different parts of that chart. As planets continue their celestial journeys, they form aspects—relationships—with the positions in your natal chart, activating new themes, lessons, and opportunities.

Think of it like this: your birth chart is the script of your life. Transits are the timing cues, telling you when it's time to act, reflect, or grow. Each planet brings a different energy:

- **Saturn** teaches responsibility and structure. Its transits can feel restrictive, but they help build lasting strength.
- **Jupiter** expands whatever it touches—bringing opportunity, but also excess if unchecked.
- **Uranus** disrupts and liberates, pushing you out of ruts and into innovation.
- **Neptune** dissolves boundaries, encouraging imagination and spiritual awakening—but can also obscure reality.
- **Pluto** transforms. Its energy is intense and regenerative, asking you to surrender what no longer serves.

Transits don't determine your fate—they illuminate the terrain. They show what areas of your life are being stirred so you can respond with awareness rather than react blindly.

---

Sarah recalled something Maya had said at a workshop: "Think of your chart as a garden. The planets are the weather. Some transits are gentle spring rains that help you bloom. Others are storms that uproot what no longer serves you. Both are necessary."

The metaphor stuck with her. It helped explain why Mars transiting her 7th house had stirred up tension in her relationship—or why, after a tough Saturn transit, she'd suddenly found clarity about her career.

Now, with Saturn approaching her Sun, Sarah knew she was entering a period of reckoning. This wasn't about punishment—it was about growth through maturity. Saturn would ask hard questions: Who are you really? What do you want to build? Where are you out of alignment with your true self?

---

Wanting clarity, she texted Maya: "What should I expect with Saturn on my Sun?"

The reply came quickly: "A redefining of your sense of self. It's time to commit to your purpose. Step into your authority."

They met the next afternoon at their usual café, cozy and warm with the scent of cinnamon and coffee in the air. "It feels like everything is about to change," Sarah said.

Maya nodded. "That's Saturn's way. It strips away illusions and demands truth. But the reward is clarity and strength. If you do the work, you'll come out the other side transformed."

---

Over the following weeks, Sarah embraced the transit as a teacher. She re-evaluated her goals. She journaled through her fears. She made peace with the idea that progress wasn't always fast—it could be slow, steady, and soul-deep.

When the conjunction finally arrived, Sarah didn't feel dread. She felt readiness. She saw how her challenges were invitations to grow. The stars weren't distant observers—they were companions, reflecting the wisdom already inside her.

---

In the next chapter, we'll explore another key celestial influence: the Moon. You'll discover how lunar cycles shape your emotions and offer powerful opportunities for healing, release, and renewal. The cosmos isn't just out there—it lives in rhythm with your own inner tides.

## 4: MOON CYCLES AND EMOTIONAL HEALING – ALIGNING WITH LUNAR ENERGY

Silver moonlight spilled through Sarah's bedroom window, casting a luminous glow across her journal. She sat cross-legged on the floor, pen poised above paper, her thoughts swirling with the same rhythm that pulled the tides. Tonight marked a full moon—a culmination she'd been tracking for weeks as she followed the lunar cycle. And now, she was ready to release.

She glanced at the calendar pinned to her wall, each phase of the moon carefully marked: New Moon, Waxing Crescent, First Quarter, Gibbous, Full Moon. Each had brought a shift in her energy and emotions. The waxing crescent had sparked ideas. The first quarter had tested her focus. The gibbous phase had pushed her to refine her intentions. Now, beneath the full moon's light, she felt called to let go of what no longer served her.

"Okay," she whispered. "Let's do this."

The moon is one of astrology's most powerful and personal influences. Its phases reflect not only changes in the sky but in our internal world—our moods, emotions, and intuitive tides. Just as the moon pulls at oceans, it also pulls at our subconscious. Learning to work with the moon's cycles can help us regulate our emotional energy, deepen self-awareness, and foster healing.

There are four main moon phases to track:

1. **New Moon** – A time of new beginnings and setting intentions. The sky is dark, and energy turns inward. This is the seed-planting phase—ideal for visualizing your goals.
2. **Waxing Moon** – As the moon grows in light, so does momentum. This is a period for taking action, building on your intentions, and overcoming resistance.
3. **Full Moon** – The peak of illumination. Emotions may run high, but clarity and culmination arrive. It's a powerful time for release—letting go of old stories, habits, or emotional baggage.
4. **Waning Moon** – As the moon wanes, energy recedes. This phase is ideal for rest, reflection, and integrating lessons. Think of it as a cosmic exhale before the cycle begins again.

Eclipses—solar or lunar—amplify the power of these phases. A new moon solar eclipse may spark dramatic beginnings, while a full moon lunar eclipse often brings fated endings or revelations.

---

Sarah flipped back through her journal, noting her intentions from the last new moon: *Practice patience. Nurture creativity. Forgive myself.* As the moon had waxed, she noticed small shifts—more ease in her morning routine, unexpected creative sparks, and emotional waves asking her to pause and reflect.

Now, on the full moon, she felt ready to release. She lit a candle and closed her eyes. With each breath, she visualized the weight of guilt and old self-criticism lifting. Then she wrote a letter to herself—not filled with goals, but forgiveness. With a deep breath, she folded the paper and burned it in a small fireproof bowl.

It felt simple. It felt sacred.

---

Later, she remembered something Maya had said: "The moon teaches us that we're always changing. That no feeling is final. It's safe to ebb and flow."

During the waning phase, Sarah turned inward. She unplugged from social media, took quiet walks, and let her emotions guide her gently inward. The waning moon became a sacred space for reflection—where healing didn't feel like work, but like remembering.

One evening, overwhelmed by sudden melancholy, she called Maya. "I thought I was getting better," she said. "But now I feel so low."

Maya's voice was calm. "That's the dark moon phase—the void before the next beginning. It's where you rest, release expectations, and listen. You're not failing. You're shedding."

---

By the time the new moon returned, Sarah felt clearer. She created a simple ritual—lighting a fresh candle, placing her hand over her heart, and writing new intentions in her journal. She didn't try to control the outcome. She simply planted seeds.

The moon had become her teacher. Each cycle reminded her that emotions were not problems to be solved, but messages to be heard. That healing didn't mean perfection—it meant presence.

In the next chapter, we'll explore how astrology can be used for deep self-reflection and personal transformation. The stars may guide us—but it's our willingness to turn inward that shapes the journey most.

## 5: USING ASTROLOGY FOR SELF-REFLECTION AND GROWTH

The morning sun filtered through the blinds, casting golden stripes across Sarah's kitchen table. She sat with a steaming mug of tea and her journal open before her, its pages crowded with notes—moon cycles, planetary transits, and thoughts from her birth chart. Each entry felt like a breadcrumb, leading her deeper into her own story.

But today felt different. It wasn't curiosity pulling her forward—it was a sense of purpose. Astrology had become more than a study. It had become a mirror.

She flipped through old pages. Themes emerged. Emotional patterns. Recurring fears. Repeating desires. The chart had offered symbols—but it was reflection that gave them life. Still, clarity wasn't always comfortable.

She sighed, pen in hand. "Where do I even begin?" she whispered.

Almost on cue, her phone buzzed with a message from Maya: "Thinking about shadow work?"

Sarah blinked. How does she always know?

"Yes," she replied. "But it's a lot."

Maya answered: "You're not meant to feel ready. Shadow work begins with showing up anyway."

---

Astrology is a tool for radical self-reflection. It reveals patterns—of thought, emotion, behavior—that we may have ignored or suppressed. It shows us our light, but also our shadow.

The shadow, as Carl Jung defined it, includes the hidden parts of ourselves—the fears, wounds, and desires we've buried. Astrology helps us shine light on those shadows through:

- **Challenging Aspects**: Squares and oppositions often reveal inner tension.
- **Difficult Transits**: Times when the universe pushes us to grow by surfacing old wounds.
- **Sensitive Houses**: The 12th house, for example, governs the subconscious, solitude, and spiritual surrender.

Consider someone with Saturn square the Moon. That aspect might indicate deep emotional insecurities—perhaps a fear of rejection, rooted in early experiences of emotional suppression. Or someone with Pluto conjunct Venus might grapple with control or intensity in relationships, often replaying power dynamics until awareness brings healing.

---

Sarah dug deeper into her chart. One aspect jumped out: Saturn square her Moon. She remembered how often she equated love with performance—as if being worthy meant being useful. Her need to "earn" love had exhausted her for years.

She began journaling:

- *What does safety mean to me?*
- *When have I felt love without needing to achieve anything?*
- *What am I afraid to feel?*

At first, the pages came slowly. But over time, her writing became freer, more honest. She noticed the voice of self-criticism softening. The chart hadn't judged her—it had simply offered a map.

---

She then explored her Mars-Neptune opposition. It explained her constant tug-of-war between inspiration and action. She dreamed vividly but struggled with follow-through. To shift this, she started a nightly ritual: lighting a candle and writing down one small, concrete step she could take the next day. It wasn't about perfection—just consistency.

Shadow work didn't mean dwelling in darkness. It meant integrating what had been hidden.

---

One evening, her sister Emily called. Their relationship had been rocky—fraught with misunderstandings. But lately, there was space to reconnect.

"I've been thinking," Emily said. "We've carried old stuff for too long. I want to let it go."

Sarah's throat tightened. For years, she'd blamed Emily. But now, through her chart, she saw her own patterns—the ways she avoided vulnerability, the ways she'd projected expectations.

"I'm sorry," she said. "I wasn't fair either. Can we start again?"

"Yeah," Emily replied softly. "Let's."

---

By embracing astrology as a mirror, Sarah discovered a truth: healing wasn't about fixing herself. It was about understanding herself—fully, compassionately.

The stars didn't dictate who she had to be. They illuminated who she already was—and who she could become.

---

In the next chapter, we'll explore one of astrology's most misunderstood phenomena: retrogrades. These cycles aren't cosmic punishment—they are invitations to pause, review, and realign with your inner truth.

## 6: THE ROLE OF RETROGRADES IN SPIRITUAL LESSONS

The first time Sarah heard the term "Mercury retrograde," she laughed. Her coworker had blamed it for a printer malfunction and a spilled coffee. "It's the planets," she'd said, as if that explained everything.

But now, with a deeper understanding of astrology, Sarah realized retrogrades weren't cosmic scapegoats—they were invitations. Gentle (and sometimes not-so-gentle) nudges to slow down, reflect, and recalibrate.

She opened her journal and wrote the words: *Mercury retrograde begins tomorrow.* Her thoughts were already turning inward.

---

In astrology, a retrograde occurs when a planet appears to move backward in the sky. This optical illusion is due to Earth's relative motion—but symbolically, retrogrades are powerful times to pause and revisit the areas of life governed by that planet.

Each planet's retrograde carries its own flavor:

- **Mercury Retrograde**: Reflection in communication, technology, travel, and contracts. A time to think before speaking, double-check details, and listen more closely.
- **Venus Retrograde**: Reassessment of love, beauty, values, and relationships. Old lovers may reappear, and unspoken feelings surface.
- **Mars Retrograde**: Review of how we assert ourselves. Motivation may feel sluggish. It's a time to realign passion with purpose.
- **Jupiter & Saturn Retrogrades**: Long-term evaluation of growth, discipline, and belief systems. Lessons resurface to be integrated.
- **Uranus, Neptune & Pluto Retrogrades**: These slower retrogrades offer deep, collective reflection. They stir spiritual, generational, and subconscious shifts.

Retrogrades are not setbacks—they're seasons of internal processing. They remind us that growth isn't always forward-moving.

---

Sarah decided to treat Mercury retrograde like a sacred retreat. She limited screen time, backed up her files, and postponed any big decisions. Instead, she focused on writing, dreaming, and reconnecting with her inner voice.

She also noticed how retrogrades affected her chart personally. Mercury was retrograding through her 4th house—the house of home, family, and inner roots. Without planning to, she found herself sorting through old photos, organizing her space, and calling her parents more often. There was a sense of emotional tidying, like preparing the soil for something new.

---

One afternoon, her internet crashed mid-Zoom meeting. Flustered, she texted Maya. "Mercury strikes again."

Maya replied: "Yes—but maybe it's asking you to take a breath. Not everything broken needs fixing right away. Sometimes the pause is the medicine."

Sarah laughed aloud. She lit a candle and sat on the couch, allowing stillness to be enough.

---

Later that week, she reread old journal entries. Buried in the pages were ideas she'd forgotten, dreams she'd shelved. One in particular caught her eye—a children's book idea she'd outlined but never pursued. Inspired, she created a new document on her laptop: *First Draft – Luna's Journey*.

The retrograde hadn't blocked her. It had returned her to herself.

---

By the time Mercury stationed direct, Sarah felt more clear, grounded, and aware. Retrograde season had shown her the power of reflection—and the wisdom in slowing down.

---

In the final chapter, we'll step back and see the full picture. We'll explore how astrology can be woven into daily life as a spiritual practice—one that connects you with your higher self, the rhythms of nature, and the divine intelligence of the cosmos.

.

# CONCLUSION: EMBRACING THE COSMIC DANCE

**Conclusion: Embracing the Cosmic Dance**

The stars no longer felt distant to Sarah. What had once been twinkling lights in the sky were now intimate companions—guides on her path of growth, healing, and awakening. She no longer looked to astrology for quick answers. Instead, she approached it with reverence—as a living dialogue between her soul and the cosmos.

On her altar sat a candle, her favorite crystal, and a printout of her birth chart. Not for prediction—but for reflection. She understood now that astrology didn't give her certainty. It gave her clarity. Not rules, but rhythms. Not fate, but freedom through awareness.

She smiled as she closed her journal, a new intention written on the page: *Keep listening.*

---

This is the heart of astrology as a spiritual practice: presence. It teaches us to observe cycles, honor intuition, and trust the unfolding of our personal evolution. As you've explored in these pages, astrology is more than a tool—it is a relationship. A sacred exchange between your inner world and the infinite sky.

To integrate astrology into daily life, consider:

- **Tracking transits** and how they affect your mood, choices, or energy levels.
- **Following the moon phases** for emotional insight and goal setting.
- **Journaling your reflections** during key planetary alignments.
- **Creating rituals** to connect with planetary or lunar energy.

- **Viewing challenges not as setbacks, but as invitations to grow.**

Most importantly, listen to yourself. Astrology is not a script to follow blindly, but a language to interpret with wisdom and compassion.

Whether you're navigating a Saturn return, embracing your lunar nature, or sitting in stillness during a retrograde, you are never disconnected from the greater whole. The universe moves with you.

You don't need to have all the answers. You just need to stay curious. Let the stars remind you of your own brilliance, and let your chart become a mirror—not of who you should be, but of who you already are.

So continue your journey with heart and humility. Let astrology be your sacred compass as you walk the path of soul growth.

The sky is always speaking.

## ABOUT THE AUTHOR

Seraphina Hartwell is a spiritual mentor, intuitive counselor, and bestselling author specializing in soul-centered living, karmic healing, and self-discovery. With over two decades of experience blending ancient wisdom traditions with modern psychology, she has helped thousands navigate life transitions, uncover hidden potentials, and align with their higher purpose.

Printed in Great Britain
by Amazon